The Ministry and Purpose of the Associate Pastor

Keep The Focus In The Ministry

Robert L. Sheppard

Copyright © 2014 by Robert L. Sheppard

The Ministry and Purpose of the Associate Pastor
Keep the focus in the Ministry
by Robert L. Sheppard

Printed in the United States of America

ISBN 9781498412735

All rights reserved solely by the author. The author guarantees all contents are original and do not infringe upon the legal rights of any other person or work. No part of this book may be reproduced in any form without the permission of the author. The views expressed in this book are not necessarily those of the publisher.

Scripture quotations taken from the King James Version (KJV) – public domain

Scripture quotations taken from the New International Version (NIV). Copyright © 1973, 1978, 1984, 2011 by Biblica, Inc.™. Used by permission. All rights reserved.

Scripture quotations taken from the New King James Version (NKJV). Copyright © 1979, 1980, 1982 by Thomas Nelson, Inc. Used by permission. All rights reserved.

www.xulonpress.com

Dedication

To my lovely wife, children and grandchildren, I thank God for you all. I pray that we will continue to grow spiritual in this life and in the generation to come.

To my parents who are deceased I thank God for them. Special thanks to my lovely mother for being my encourager.

TABLE OF CONTENTS

Dedication................................v
Acknowledgments.........................ix
Introduction.............................xi

1. The Church Age 15
2. Leading Others 23
3. The Call of the Associate Pastor 29
4. Burnout 33
5. Character Counts..................... 41
6. Understanding Your Role 49
7. Develop Leadership Skills 57
8. The Life of Godliness 65
9. Maintain a Spirit of Humility 71
10. Biblical Principles for Leadership........ 77

Conclusion 85
Questions for Review:.................... 87
Bibliography 89

Acknowledgments

I am forever grateful for the blessings, love grace and mercy shown to me by God the Father, God the Son, and God the Holy Spirit. I am forever thankful for the guidance of the Holy Spirit. He guided my thoughts and granted me wisdom, knowledge, and understanding to fulfill my dream of writing this book.

Introduction

A legitimate question may be asked, "Is the subject of leadership biblical? Can we study the Bible and find methods to guide our thinking?" The answer is yes, if we have an open mind to perceive its insights. Every basic honorable principle of leadership and management has its root and foundation in the Word of God. The Bible is filled with examples of God searching for leaders. When they were found they were used to the full limit as they met his spiritual requirements, despite their human failings.[1]

The ministry is about serving others. One must be God centered and people focused to be a servant. Associate pastors are servants. They embrace the

---

[1] Ted W. Engstrom, the Making of a Christian Leader (Grand Rapids, Michigan The Zondervan Corporation, 1976) 25, 26

biblical principles to, "love God and love one another." In this book I will point out from a biblical perspective the purpose and ministry of associate pastors. They are ministers who occupy the chairs in the pulpit alongside the senior pastor. Not all churches have this arrangement. Their purpose and mission is to assist the senior pastor in carrying out the mission of the local church. The root beginning of the associate leader can be traced back to the biblical days.

Assistants have been assigned to walk alongside leaders since the days of the Old Testament. Abraham had a faithful servant, Eliezer of Damascus, whom he trust with his whole household including selecting a wife for his son Isaac (Genesis 24:1-4 KJV). Moses' brother Aaron was the first high priest of Israel. Aaron's sons served as priests under his leadership. They administered the spiritual matters of the tabernacle and ministered to the people of God.

> **One must be God centered and people focused to be a servant.**

In the twenty-first century, associate pastors assist senior pastors in accomplishing the mission and ministry of the church to present the plan of salvation. Serving as an associate pastor is a position of servant hood that can be joyful and meaningful.

Chapter 1
The Church Age

The church age began in the first century on the day of Pentecost in the book of (Acts 2:1-47 KJV). The Greek term for church *ecclesia* means "called out ones gathered together to serve and accomplish a mission."[2] It is an organism and an organization that is designed to grow as it reverences and praises God. "Praising God and having favor with all people; and the Lord added to the church daily such as should be saved" (Acts 2:47 KJV). The church is an organized spiritual entity that has a hierarchy of leaders and subordinates. The church is to function under the tutelage of the God-head—God the Father, God the Son, and God the Holy Spirit.

---

[2] wTed W. Engstrom, the Making of a Christian Leader (Grand Rapids, Michigan The Zondervan Corporation, 1976) 25, 26

Jesus is head of the church. He gave his life for the church. The Holy Bible gives scriptural directives for guiding and leading the church. The Bible is the only written methodology God uses to relate to man. It is the only tool that is effective for carrying out the mission of the church.

Pastors, associates, and saints are servants that carry out the mission of the church. Pastors are the under-shepherds of the local church. They are the ones God calls to lead and prepare the saints to be instruments of obedience in fulfilling the commission given to the church by Jesus before his ascension. We are to, "Go into all the world, and preach the gospel to every creature" (Mark 16:15 KJV). Associate Pastors are to assist the senior pastor in fulfilling the mission of the church.

The Hierarchy of the Church

In the hierarchy of the local church, the senior pastor is the leader in charge of all ministries. Associate pastors are needed to assist in carrying out these ministries especially in the large and mega churches where there are many ministries that have to be fulfilled. In laboring Jesus speaks of a harvest, then said He unto His disciples "The harvest truly is plenteous, but the laborers are few". "Therefore pray the Lord of the harvest to send out laborers." "The harvest in laboring." (Matthew 9: 37-38 KJV) Associate pastors are laborers that are needed to meet the needs of any diverse congregation.

Megachurches are constantly receiving new members from different racial, social, educational, and economical backgrounds. Many large and mega churches provide in reach, outreach ministries to their congregation and communities as well. This includes feeding the hungry, shelters for the homeless, evangelism, giving educational and financial assistance, visiting the sick, and ministering in nursing homes, jails and prisons. One or more of the listed ministries are often assigned to the associate pastor for leadership oversight.

> **An effective associate pastor must see himself as a foot soldier enlisted in the army of God.**

Associate pastors must be willing to help facilitate the mission of the church and be able to teach the plan of salvation in a way that touches the lives and souls of the congregation. This is especially true for believers that have a sincere heart the desire for attending Bible studies. Many congregants that attend Bible studies have a thirst, and hunger for the Word of God. Sometime senior pastors can become overwhelmed with the multiple ministries of the church, when this occur they can delegate certain responsibilities to the associate pastor as they work to meet all the ministry needs of the congregation. Pastor know that if the congregant's lives are not touched spiritually, they will seek a new congregation elsewhere.

Any person holding the important position of associate pastor in the church must be born again and baptized in the name of the Father, of the Son and of the Holy Spirit, and have a clear understanding of God's Word.

Focus on Ministry

In order for the church to continually offer the plan of salvation and meet the needs of the congregation, the senior pastor needs to involve the associate pastor effectively in the ministry. When an associate pastor is placed in a ministry to make a difference, one will grow and become more confident. For example, in some congregation where young people are not supervise properly an associate pastor maybe assign to take control of an unruly situation, calm behaviors that was once considered uncontrollable. When an associate pastor control situations that were once uncontrollable one may see oneself as an effective foot soldier enlisted in the army of God. Associate pastors must accept and know their ministry, and be focused on the ministry or ministries assigned to them.

For example, as an associate pastor I teach a Bible study, a Sunday school class, and (B. T. U.) Baptist Training Union. I realize that one needs ample time to prepare for each class. I begin my studies with prayer and mediating. I understand and know that one need time for reading, studying, and research. My desire is to be an effective teacher and perform at a high level of proficiency and do what is expected of me.

As associate pastors, it is important to understand we are to do our very best, but we are not to attempt to overshadow upstage or usurp the senior pastor's authority. While serving as an associate pastor on the pastoral staff of a local church in St. Petersburg, Florida, I always do my best knowing I was divine called, commissioned by God to serve and assist the senior pastor of this church.

I understood that in order to be an effective spiritual leader, I shall always stay focused on what I was called to do. I will keep a mindset of humility, possess a sincere desire to serve God, and seek to truly understand my position within the hierarchy of the church. My perspective from several years of experience in the local church is that my first line of leadership began within my home with my own family. Though I am not suggesting that one cannot be an effective leader unless one is a parent, I have learned that my wife and children bring out the best leadership qualities I have within me. The Apostle Paul stated, "For if a man know not how to rule his own house, how shall he take care of the church of God?" (1 Timothy 3:5 NKJV).

I have learned from reading various biblical resources and text-books, that the Bible is the best resource for learning effective spiritual leadership principles. The Old and New Testaments give many examples of assistant leaders who were faithful to their leaders, and obedient to the Word of God. The Bible also gives examples of those who were rebellious against their leaders, and were not obedient to the Word of God. We can learn a lot from studying both of these groups.

☙ Key Points from Chapter 1

- ☙ An effective associate pastor must see himself as a foot soldier enlisted in the army of God.
- ☙ To be an effective spiritual leader, we must always be focused on what we are called to do, have a mindset of humility, possess a sincere desire to serve God, and seek to truly understand our position within the hierarchy of the church.

Chapter 2

Leading Others

Leading others requires knowing scriptures, biblical principles acquiring and fine tuning one's skills. Associate pastors are leaders within the church and need the desire to become effective servant leaders. Leadership qualities have to be developed through teaching, training, encouraging, and being given responsibilities through assisting the senior pastor in meeting the needs of the congregation. Spiritual leadership abilities grow as a result of listening, getting involved, and associating with experienced established leaders. Associate pastors must be willing to dedicate time to reading and studying to develop an understanding of God's word. Apostle Paul Admonished Timothy to "Study

> **Associate pastors should always seek guidance from the Holy Spirit.**

to shew thyself approved unto God, a workman that needeth not to be ashamed, rightly dividing the word of truth" (2Timothy 2:15 KJV).

Maturity comes through exposure to challenges and life experiences in addition to being around experienced leadership. Maturity and wisdom do not automatically come because you are in a leadership position. Wisdom is an effective tool. It can be effective when leading others. According to scripture, "If any of you lacks wisdom, he should ask God, who gives generously to all without finding fault" (James 1:5 NIV). Therefore, associate pastors should always seek guidance from the Holy Spirit.

Good leadership abilities and qualities are quickly observed by local church officers and members. Premium traits that others look for in assessing spiritual leaders are good behavior, trustfulness, faithfulness, compassion, and the love of God's word. Associates pastors must have a positive attitude and a spirit of cooperation to occupy the second chair in the church's hierarchy. The seats on the platform are reserved for those who are serious about the ministries of our Lord and Savior Jesus Christ. On many occasions associate pastors subsequently become senior pastors themselves.

Scripture encourages us as associate pastors to be patient because God knows our purpose. He is the one that placed us and called us to be an associate pastor. The Apostle Paul encourages us as he did the Philippians by saying, "Being confident of this very thing, that which he hath begun a good work in you will perform it until the day of Jesus Christ" (Philippians 1:6 NKJV). We can be confident in our ministry when we know our spiritual gift and purpose, whether it is teaching, administration, or using any other God given talent.

> **God is the one that placed us and called us to be an associate pastor.**

We should realize God is doing a work in and through us. We should not be too anxious about promotion knowing God will promote us when the time comes. "For promotion comes neither from the east, nor from the west, nor from the south, but God is the judge: "He puts down one, and sets up another" (Psalm 75:6-7 NKJV). The success of any local church depends on the positive support and cooperation of not only the associate pastor, but is inclusive of the whole church.

Everyone that is a member of the church must have the mindset to encourage one another regardless of what position they occupy within their local church. It is a blessing for everyone in the congregation when believers encourage one another in the ministry and continuously focus on God's Word and do His will.

The Three C's of Effective Leadership

The three C's of being an effective leader are Commitment, Communication, and Cooperation. Commitment is being involved mentally, physically, and spiritually in the vision of the church. It is a pledge or agreement with that vision. It facilitates our minds to implement action by reasoning, thinking, understanding, and applying the wisdom and knowledge needed to see that the vision is fulfilled. It reminds us that we should always be fully engaged in our ministry.

Communication is the ability to express ourselves clearly through teaching, preaching, and verbal interaction with others. Cooperation is the unity of a group of people acting as one with the same goal in mind. Each member of the leadership team must possess all of these qualities in order for the ministry to function efficiently and effectively.

☞ Key Points from Chapter 2

- ☞ Associate pastors should always seek guidance from the Holy Spirit.
- ☞ God is the one that placed us and called us to be an associate pastor.
- ☞ The three C's of being an effective leader are Commitment, Communication, and Cooperation.

CHAPTER 3

THE CALL OF THE ASSOCIATE PASTOR

Associate pastors are called with an efficacious call to help disseminate and spread the teachings of Jesus Christ, and to assist the senior pastor in the mission of the church. It is feasible and practical for all local churches to have an associate pastor. In today's local churches with various out-reach and in-reach- ministries to fulfill no single senior pastor has the capability or time to interact with every member of the congregation.

The senior pastor does more than teach and preach. He is the head administrator of every ministry within the church. He is responsible for the smooth operation of the church and everyone that is paid for services rendered such as secretaries, janitors, groundskeepers, and other office workers. He is also the primary counselor for members of the congregation that are going through sickness, death, marital issues, and couples about to be married. Without sufficient pastoral support, congregational problems can create a short tenure for senior pastors.

Associate pastors are invaluable servants to the local church. There are few books, pamphlets, magazines, and periodic-articles that offer guidance and insights into this important position. Though some associate pastors may receive pay for their work, it is probable that this position is looked upon as temporary. The associate pastor is quite often in training to transition to the position of senior pastor though this is not always true. Some associate pastors will never become a senior pastor.

> **The position of associate pastor should be looked at as a privilege and is a call to servant hood.**

The associate pastor position is unlike the senior pastor's position in that the associate pastor does not have direct authority. His authority is delegated and he takes directive from the senior pastor. The position of associate pastor should be looked at as a privilege and is a call to servant hood.

Within this position of servant hood, an associate pastor must emulate and produce the fruit of the Holy Spirit as listed in (Galatians 5:22-23 KJV).

> *But the fruit of the Spirit is love, joy, peace, longsuffering, gentleness, goodness, faith, meekness, temperance: against such there is no law.*

The associate pastor is carefully selected by the senior pastor to be of service to the church and congregation by assisting the senior pastor in any way needed to meet the needs and challenges of senior leadership.

Key Points from Chapter 3

- The position of associate pastor should be looked at as a privilege and is a call to servant hood.
- Within this position of servant hood, an associate pastor must emulate and produce the fruit of the Holy Spirit as listed in (Galatians 5:22-23 KJV).

Chapter 4

Burnout

Many senior pastors in local churches have become aware of the enormous challenges that have to be faced on a daily basis in a growing congregation. Inadequate help and overwhelming congregational challenges can cause discouragement for the senior pastor. Some may even quit the ministry altogether and seek other professions. Help is needed to alleviate burnout and early retirement. Burnout is not a new problem within leadership. It was noticed and dealt with in the Old Testament.

An effective leader must have an open mind to listen and accept advice.

Moses

Moses was a leader appointed by God to lead the Israelites to the Promised Land. He judged the Israelites from morning to evening, and as a result he became overwhelmed with their problems. He got to the point he was failing as a leader.

> *So Moses' father-in-law said to him, "The thing that you do is not good. Both you and these people who are with you will surely wear yourselves out. For this thing is too much for you; you are not able to perform it by yourself. Listen now to my voice; I will give you counsel, and God will be with you: Stand before God for the people, so that you may bring the difficulties to God."*
> (Exodus 18:17-19 NKJV)

Moses' father-in-law realized the problem and approached Moses to give good counsel. Moses accepted his father-in-law Jethro's advice and implemented the needed change. Moses' ability to listen and obey sound advice made him a successful leader.

> *And Moses chose able men out of all Israel, and made them heads over the people: rulers of thousands, rulers of hundreds, rulers of fifties, and rulers of tens. So they judged the people at all times; the hard cases they brought to Moses, but they judged every small case themselves.* (Exodus 18:25-26 NKJV).

When a person is in a leadership position he must not be of the opinion, "I am always right." An effective leader must have an open mind to listen and accept advice. "Moses was a very meek man above all the men who were upon the face of the earth" (Numbers 12:3 NKJV). He had personal challenges and became frustrated on occasion while leading the Israelites. While they were traveling through the wilderness, Moses was instructed by God to speak to the rock to bring water to the thirsty Israelites, but instead he struck the rock twice (Numbers 20:11 NKJV). Frustration and burnout can occur in today's senior pastor as well.

Church deacons and officials are aware of potential pastor burnout and the importance of finding good associate pastors to assist their senior pastor. Mega-churches particularly need effective associate pastors. Many mega churches have a congregation membership as high as ten-thousand, some have even more. They hire associate pastors and pay them a salary. Many associate pastors in mega churches have graduated from college and seminary and have advanced degrees in ministry. They are employed by the church and work forty hours a week. This is not always true for churches with small congregations who want their associate pastors to volunteer their time.

Volunteerism is necessary in small churches or they would not be able to carry out all their ministries. Many small local churches would not be able to meet the needs of the congregation successfully without voluntarism especially if they cannot afford to pay their associate pastors. Allegiance to the faith and voluntarism of the associate pastor help keep the local church moving forward with their mission to offer the plan of salvation and other needed ministries to their congregation.

The Associate pastor must always remember the way we treat people must not be motivated by what they can do for us but by love. We are called to love, serve people, and not to determine whether they deserve to be loved or not. Our knowledge of the scriptures, teaches us compassion toward others, obedience to God, faithful in prayer, a godly character, and a willingness to serve.

The position of an associate pastor is by no means trivial, inferior or placed low on the totem pole of ministry. It is highly spiritual and very important. It should be recognized for the contribution that the associate pastor brings to the congregation. Good associate pastors are invaluable to the church and senior pastor. Many associate pastors holding this second position are very capable, extremely qualified, and have the potential to become a great future leader.

Joshua

A good example is Joshua who was an assistant that God promoted to succeed Moses as leader over the Israelites.

> *Moses my servant is dead. Now then you and all these people, get ready to cross the Jordan River into the land I am about to give them to the Israelites."* (Joshua 1:2 NIV).

> *"Be strong and courageous, because you will lead these people to inherit the land I swore to their forefathers to give them." (Joshua 1:6 NIV).*

Joshua was a successful leader. He was faithful, wholly trusted, and believed in God. He had a positive attitude as an assistant to Moses. According to Martin E. Hawkins, God calls some people to train for the pastorate through the assistant role: Using the assistance role as training for the senior pastorate should not diminish the position and make it "second fiddle."[3]

Joshua was a patient assistant leader, truthful, obedient to his call, and not willing to go along with the crowd. He did not compromise his faith even when others saw things differently. He was one of the two spies who brought back a positive report that the people of Israel could defeat the people in the land of Canaan.

Joshua was an intern under Moses not knowing that he was going to be the future leader of Israel. God deemed it necessary to put Joshua in this position for training and preparation for the future challenges he would face as a leader. Leadership can be challenging; therefore, proper preparation and training are a necessary part of the process to becoming effective.

Competent leaders make a significant difference in the lives of people that are being led. It is a privilege to be called to be an associate to a senior pastor who is a competent and strong leader. To be ready when the opportunity comes, we need to prepare by taking advantage of the academic training available,

---

[3] Martin E. Hawkins, the Associate Pastor (Published & Holman Publishers Nashville Tennessee. 2005), 36, 37.

be diligent in study, and be serious about the ministry. Study plays an indispensable role in the associate pastor's overall role in the ministry. Biblical knowledge and theological accuracy are a vitally important aspect of a leader's training so they can correctly interpret and teach the truth of Scripture. The Holy Spirit gives us the ability and understanding to carry out the mandate of the Great Commission whether we are a senior or an associate pastor.

⌁ Key Points from Chapter 4

- ⌁ An effective leader must have an open mind to listen and accept advice.
- ⌁ Associate pastors are to have a love for all people, a knowledge of the scriptures, compassion toward others, obedience to God, be faithful in prayer, have a godly character, and a willingness to serve.
- ⌁ Biblical knowledge and theological accuracy are a vitally important aspect of a leader's training so they can correctly interpret and teach the truth of Scripture.

Chapter 5

Character Counts

Character reflects our conduct. Character really counts when it comes to being an associate pastor. The message of salvation is understood better by believers and nonbelievers when they see the godly character and conduct of the associate pastor. Character that is godly reinforces what the church and pastor are teachings and gives a strong witness to what they read in the Scriptures. Characteristics that are ungodly are noticed by saints as well.

> **The message of salvation is understood better by believers and nonbelievers when they see the godly character and conduct of the associate pastor.**

God's Word lights the way

Associate pastors must keep their character in check at all times in order to perform ministry in a godly manner. The best way to keep the mind focused is through continuous pray, study, reliance on the Scriptures, and living a life that truly reflects the teachings of Jesus Christ. The life walk of the associate pastor should always shine forth the light of God and His word. When associates pastors walk in the light there is obvious obedience, faith, righteousness, agreement, compassion, and understanding of God's Word. The light of God's Word gives guidance and direction,"Thy Word is a lamp unto my feet and a light to my path" (Psalm 119:105 KJV).

Associate pastors must live a sanctified life and particularly exemplify the high moral standards that are required by God of all saints. As the associate pastor expresses these attributes in fellowship and interaction with others, they are indicators he is serious about the ministry, secure in who he is in God, stable in the position God has called him to, and satisfied with doing the work of ministry in his assigned position.

Associate pastors must avoid immoral behavior at all times. Any form of immoral behavioral activities such as substance abuse, drugs, alcohol or sexual misbehavior will often start gossip and bring discredit to not only the associate pastor's reputation and character, but to the church as well. Associate pastors should always be aware of this and must avoid any situation that might reflect negative behavior on himself or the congregation.

> **When associate pastors walk in the light there is obvious obedience, faith, righteousness, agreement, compassion, and understanding of God's Word.**

Submission

Associate pastors must exhibit submission to their leadership. In the body of Christ, submission gives evidence of a humble heart and a spirit filled life. It is also an indication of how willing a person is to accept guidance and directives from the senior pastor. Submission is not a characteristic of weakness, but of strength, faith, obedience, and spiritual growth. Submission is one of the core values exhibited by anyone who has been born again. The spirit of submission exhibited by the associate pastor will be noticed by the senior pastor and the saints within the church.

It is impossible for an associate pastor or any person for that matter to perform the ministry of Jesus Christ without submission to the leadership God places over us. Scripture brings attention to this principle.

> **Submission is not a characteristic of weakness, but of strength, faith, obedience, and spiritual growth.**

Ministering "remember them which have the rule over you, who have spoke unto you the word of God; whose faith follow, considering the end of their conversation" (Hebrews 13:7).

The Holy Spirit is the power within you that drives your willing submission to authority. Jesus, though he was the Son of God, did not consider himself above submission. He humbled and submitted himself to be baptized by John the Baptist (Matthew 3:15 KJV). Jesus is always our best example of servant leadership. Submission is the will of God (Mark 3:35 KJV).

Submission is one of the main ingredients of being a true servant of the Lord. It determines what one does and how one acts in certain situations concerning ones ministry. Submission builds associate pastors credibility and earns the trust of those around them.

> **Jesus is always our best example of servant leadership.**

Maturity is another characteristic that associate pastors must have. Maturity does not necessary apply to an associate pastor's chronological age. It applies to being spiritual mature in regard to growth in becoming more and more Christ like. Associate pastors must be spiritually mature in order to be effective leaders.

Novice

A novice is a new believer in the faith and not mature in the knowledge of the Word of God. He or she has no experience or time in the ministry. The Apostle Paul points out that a leader in ministry: "not a novice, lest being lifted up with pride he fall into the condemnation of the devil" (1 Timothy 3:6 KJV). A novice is easily persuaded to accept outside influence and should not be elevated too quickly to assume a position of leadership.

Along with the maturity comes the ability to effectively communicate the truth of God's Word. This plays an important role in effective ministry. Associate pastors must be able to communicate truthfully and compassionately. Misspoken words or words spoken in a negative sense will create misunderstanding. Associate pastors must guard their conversations so as not to cause confusion among others. If associate pastors treat their conversations seriously, so will others.

Associate pastors should not be talkative nor engage in unproductive conservation. "Avoid godless chatter, because those who indulge in it will become more and more ungodly" (2 Timothy 2:16 NIV).

Associate pastors should not speak about things they do not know or manipulate words to impress others. Associate pastors must engage others carefully in conversations according to God's instructions, "Let your speech be always with grace, seasoned with salt, that ye may know how ye ought to answer every man" (Colossians 4:6 KJV).

Associate pastors should learn to speak the truth in love to help others mature in ministry as well.

> *Instead, speaking the truth in love, we will grow to become in every respect the mature body of him who is the head, that is, Christ.* (Ephesians 4:15 NIV)

❧ Key Points from Chapter 5

- ❧ The message of salvation is understood better by believers and nonbelievers when they see the godly character and conduct of the associate pastor.
- ❧ When associate pastors walk in the light there is obvious obedience, faith righteousness, agreement compassion, and understanding of God's Word.

- Submission to the authority placed over us is not a characteristic of weakness, but of strength, faith, obedience, and spiritual growth.
- Jesus is always our best example of servant leadership.

CHAPTER 6

Understanding Your Role

It is important that associate pastors understand their role as helpers to the senior pastor and the congregation. Associate pastoral duties in churches may vary but here is a basic list:

1. Preach the Word as called upon by the senior Pastor.
2. Assist in administering the Lord's Supper.
3. Assist in the baptizing of new members.
4. Be a strong prayer leader.
5. Teach a Bible study and Sunday school classes as needed.
6. Visit sick members of the congregation.

7. Lead and oversee outreach ministry to communities.
8. Attend church business meetings.
9. Support activities of the congregation.
10. Assist with funerals, wakes, and memorial services.
11. Pursue continuing education through seminary and church workshops.
12. Support in reach and outreach ministries of the church.

Associate pastors should be cooperative and perform every assigned ministry with passion and enthusiasm. Associate pastors must understand the priority of the church that was set by Jesus Christ in the four Gospels.

"Follow me" is a command spoken by Jesus to the disciples and the church. The gospel of Matthew particularly brings clarity to Jesus' command to follow Him. Bill Hull explains that (Matthew 28:19-20

KJV) gives us the blueprint, the method, and the methodology for fulfilling Christ command.[4]

> *Go ye therefore, and teach all nations, baptizing them in the name of the Father, and of the Son, and of the Holy Ghost: Teaching them to observe all things whatsoever I have commanded you: and, lo, I am with you always, even unto the end of the world. Amen.*

Church Decorum

Associate pastors are to assist the senior pastor with church decorum. The purpose of church decorum is to keep order and discipline within the congregation. Decorum constitutes the wellbeing of the congregation and enhances spiritual growth for all. Jesus tells the church how to treat disorderly believers in Scriptures the congregation, "And if he shall neglect to hear them, tell it unto the church: but

---

4 Bill Hull, The disciple making Pastor (Grand Rapids, Michigan Baker Books, 2008) 68

if he neglect to hear the church, let him be unto the as a heathen and a publican" (Matthew 18:17 NKJV). The Apostle Paul instructs us to let all things in the church be done decently and in order (1 Corinthians 14:40 NKJV).

Committed to the Vision

Associate pastors must support the senior pastor's vision and not be a stumbling block. The vision of the senior pastor must be known to all of the church. It must be repeated constantly by the associate pastor so that all members of the congregation are fully aware of it. Associate pastors should lead the charge with enthusiasm showing they are in agreement with the senior pastor's vision so that members of the church will be inspired.

Associate pastors must commit to the senior pastor's God given vision without wanting to change or discourage it. The pastor's vision is more important than any personal ego or agenda. Associate pastors must remember God's vision for the church is divinely given to the senior pastor. They must have the mindset that as they help the senior pastor with the vision for the church they are learning how to relate more closely with other members of the congregation with different personalities, thoughts, and ideas.

Vision for the church is usually carried out in steps. After each step is agreed upon the next one is implemented until the vision is completed. Often the associate pastor is involved in implementing these steps which makes it so vitally important that he is fully and enthusiastically supporting it.

The commitment to support the senior pastor's vision gives associates pastors experience and a model to follow as well. Regardless of how proficient associate pastors might be, there is always a new skill to be learned in the ministry. The opportunity and exposure of working directly with the senior pastor to achieve his vision is a blessing within itself. Associate pastors can learn new skills and techniques as they assist their senior pastor in the realization of his God given vision. New leadership skills can be shared with others and put to the test. It is important that associate pastors be opened minded, teachable, and willing learners as well. They must possess a cooperative attitude and be a team player.

Known by His Fruit

> *You will know them by their fruits. Do men gather grapes from thorn bushes or figs from thistles?* (Matthew 7:16 NKJV)

A positive reputation is expected of associate pastors. Scripture teaches that people are known by the fruit they bear. It is obvious that one's fruit (behavior) can create a good or bad reputation. It is the prerogative of the senior pastor to give the associate pastor their assignments. When associate pastors practice their roles as reputable helpers to senior pastors, the whole church will see that they have their minds focused on the Lord's work.

Associate pastors must remember their call to the ministry is about the Great Commission. They must perform to the best of their ability and be grateful for the opportunity to serve the Lord in the position of associate pastor. Associate pastors should not be short sighted or pessimistic in their approach to ministry. They should continue to develop good work ethics and engage in positive dialogue with the senior pastor and the congregation.

☞ Key Points from Chapter 6

- ☞ Associate pastors should be cooperative and perform every assigned ministry with passion and enthusiasm.
- ☞ Assisting the senior pastor with church decorum constitutes the wellbeing of the congregation and enhances spiritual growth for all.
- ☞ Associate pastors must commit to the senior pastor's God given vision without wanting to change or discourage it.
- ☞ It is important that associate pastors be opened minded, teachable, and willing learners

Chapter 7
Develop Leadership Skills

The development of leadership skills is continuous and progressive. Associate pastors are Christian leaders. In order to lead others, they must learn and develop relationship skills. This means that associate pastors must be trained, allowed time to grow, develop, and mature. The senior pastor must not select an associate pastor based on nepotism or personal friendship. Favoritism is inconsistent with the Scripture "My brethren do not hold the faith of our Lord Jesus Christ the Lord of glory with partiality" (James 2: 1 NKJV). The senior pastor must recognize potential leadership abilities in his choice of an associate pastor. This is vitally and important to the mission of the church. The senior pastor is also responsible for training and placing the associate pastor in the right place where he will grow and mature.

Associate pastors must realize that there is always more to be learned even after they have achieved a level of leadership skill. Leadership is a never ending learning process because it is always evolving. Leadership training and development requires accountability to determine faithfulness, productivity, and to make necessary adjustments relative to what is being done incorrectly or ineffectively in the ministry responsibilities one is given.

> **Leadership is a never ending learning process because it is always evolving.**

Accountability and Faithfulness

Jesus gives an illustration of accountability and responsibility in the parable of the three servants who were given a mission to invest their master's money. The three were given different amounts of money according to their individual abilities. Each servant was free to invest as he pleased. Two of the servants invested wisely and one did not. The one that did not invest wisely was rejected and called lazy. He did not have the best interests of his master in mind (Matthew 25:15-25 NKJV).

The Apostle Paul brings to our attention the importance of being faithful in doing good work. Every believer's work is seen by God regardless of what position one may hold. Scripture says a believer's work will be tested by fire to determine their reward

> **Every believer's work is seen by God regardless of what position they may hold.**

"If anyone's work which he has built on it endures, he will receive a reward" (1 Corinthians 3:14 NKJV).

The challenges that will occur in leadership are learning tools that help in the development of leadership skills. These challenges may include conflict, hardship, and disappointment. A leader who learns to stay on the positive side of these challenges will find that their ministry is full of joy and they will experience satisfaction from a job well done. When challenges occur it is important to remember what Jesus said to His disciples in (Matthew 16:24

NKJV), "If any man will come after Me, let him deny himself and take up his cross and follow Me" (also in Luke 14:27 NKJV).

A Clear Job Description

> **Challenges that occur are learning tools that help in the development of leadership skills.**

It is necessary that associate pastors get a clear understanding of their ministry description from the senior pastor. Job descriptions are important because everyone involved needs to know what each person on the leadership team is required to do, and the expectations of what the end results should be. When each leader has a clear understanding of their job description it will greatly lessen the potential for misunderstanding within the leadership team, and everyone will benefit.

The main objectives of the associate pastor are to relieve the senior pastor of some of his ministry responsibilities and to assure that any assigned ministry is done correctly and timely.

The following factors are necessary for developing effective associate pastors:

- *Leadership ability*
- *Teachable and humble*
- *Committed to reading and studying the scriptures*
- *Good listening and communication skills*
- *Supportive of others on the leadership team*
- *Enthusiastic in carrying out each assignment*
- *Faithful to the vision of the church*

In addition to these basic leadership tools, the associate pastor must be willing to grow and develop more skills as he faces new challenges within his leadership responsibilities. It is very important that associate pastors stay informed of the on-going functions of the church so they can make intelligent and efficient decisions that involve their assigned ministries.

Secular versus Spiritual Leadership Mindsets

Associate pastors should be aware of and understand the difference between the secular and spiritual mindset of leadership.

Secular Leadership	Spiritual Leadership
Critical of others	Encourage others
Unfriendly	Seek fellowship/Compassionate
Dictator	Servant hood
Self-serving	Seek God's will
Assertive	Humble
Independent	Depends on God

It is imperative that associate pastors, read, know, and understand the biblical principles of leadership as taught in the Pastoral Epistles: 1 Timothy, 2 Timothy, and Titus. These three Epistles are highly regarded by the church to direct, select, and guide leaders.

⛌Key Points from Chapter 7

- ⛌ The development of leadership skills is continuous and progressive.
- ⛌ Leadership is a never ending learning process that it is always evolving.
- ⛌ Every believer's work is seen by God regardless of what position they may hold.
- ⛌ Challenges that occur are learning tools that help in the development of leadership skills.

Chapter 8

The Life of Godliness

The life of godliness has to be done with the right spirit; that is in the Spirit of Christ. Associate pastors must pursue their ministry in a way that brings glory to God. Whatever activity they do for the Lord, it must be done with the pursuit of godliness in mind. Even when Daniel was in captivity to the Babylonians, he still pursued the excellence of God through prayer, faith, hope, and optimism. Daniel's godly spirit was noticed by the king's officials and it was reported to the King of Babylon. As a result he was elevated to a high position. "Then this Daniel was preferred above the presidents and princes, because an excellent spirit was in him; and the king thought to set him over the whole realm" (Daniel 6:3 KJV).

When ministry is done in the spirit of godliness you will succeed. Associate pastors are to pursue their ministry with a spirit of godly excellence that will lead to positive and productive results. The best way to achieve an excellent godly spirit in ministry of any kind is to know and learn all you can about your particular area of giftedness.

It is very important to understand there are no short cuts or fast tracts in effective leadership development. Looking for a short cut or a fast tract leads to ineffective preparation and lack of productivity. Jesus personally trained His disciples for three years. He gradually increased their spiritual growth and the understanding of ministering by sending them among the ungodly. "Behold, I send you as sheep in the midst of wolves therefore be shrewd as serpents and harmless as doves" Matthew 10:16 NKJV). This verse is a warning that the associate pastor will sometimes have to face fierce opposition while ministering to others.

> **There are no short cuts or fast tracts in effective leadership development.**

The Process of Ordination

Ordination affirms an associate pastor's spiritual growth and maturity. It indicates the associate pastor has developed the leadership and spiritual abilities to hold the office of a church leader. The concept of ordaining men is found in the Old and New Testaments.

The process of ordination in the New Testament Church is described to Timothy, "neglect not the gift that is in thee, which was given thee by prophecy, with the laying on of the hands of the presbytery" (1 Timothy 4:14 KJV). The candidates for ordination are asked questions that will affirm their belief in the doctrines of Christianity. Biblical knowledge and theological accuracy are important prerequisites for ordination because these attributes are required for teaching the Scriptures.

The candidate is ordained through a process of lying on of hands by pastors and elders which validates the candidate's ordination, acceptance and approval. The ordination process can different within church organizations and denominations. When an associate pastor reaches the level of ordination, he is generally considered ready for a pastorate position.

The Pursuit of Godliness

The pursuit of godliness includes the associate pastors' personal life as well as his public life. His personal life must be one of being sexually pure and devoted to one wife. His personal life must not be scandalized by a past mistress and illegitimate children. God's standard are high and any immoral behavior is an abomination unto Him. An associate pastor's personal life must comply with the gospel he preaches. He must be sound in biblical doctrine, have love and compassion in his heart for God's people, and constant live an exemplary life.

> **Associate pastors must remember their calling is divine. They must exhibit the spirit of Jesus Christ their Lord and savior.**

Associate pastors must pursue godliness by practicing congeniality. They must not express disdain for another or have a narcissistic inclination to hurt others because of grudges, jealousy, anger, hate, and unforgiveness for what has occurred in the past. They must trust and rely on the safe guards of scripture. Jesus told his disciples that men would know them by their love and respect for one another. "By this shall all men know that you are my disciples, if you have love for one to another" (John13:35 NKJV). Associate pastors must remember their calling is divine. They must exhibit the spirit of Jesus Christ their Lord and savior.

✥ Key Points from Chapter 8

- ✥ There are no short cuts or fast tracts in effective leadership development.
- ✥ Associate pastors must remember their calling is divine.
- ✥ They must exhibit the spirit of Jesus Christ their Lord and savior.

Chapter 9
Maintain a Spirit of Humility

Humility is the apex of an associate pastor's character. It is a spiritual standard where a believer submits to the divine will of God at all times regardless of the situation or place they may be. "He hath shew thee, O man what is good; and what doth the Lord require of thee but to do justly, and to love mercy, and to walk humbly with thy God" (Micah 6:8 KJV).

Humility can be an issue for believers as well as nonbelievers. There is no doubt that one's environment can be a factor that helps shape humility in a person's life. A person often develops humility as a child when they are taught to be humble, polite, and respectful. However, some children are not taught any form of humility or respect. Those that are not taught humility are often negative, aggressive, rude, and disrespectful.

When believers come into the body of Christ with humility issues, these issues have to be corrected before they can live a life of true servant hood to the Lord. If an associate pastor has any form of behavior weakness, they must draw closer to the Lord through study of the Word of God, and diligently pray for a change within their heart.

> **Pride is a symptom that shows a lack of humility.**

Pride is a symptom that shows a lack of humility. One cannot go too far in leadership being prideful. Pride is one of the six things God hates that are listed in (Proverbs 6:17 KJV). Proud is a hindrance to spiritual growth as explained by Apostle Peter, "For God resists the proud and gives grace to the humble" (1 Peter 5:5b).

The Apostle Paul had an issue with pride and developed hatred for the followers of Jesus Christ before he was saved. In fact he diligently and enthusiastically persecuted the church. "As for Saul he made havoc of the church, entering into every house and dragging off men and woman committed them to prison" (Acts 8:3 NKJV). After Paul's encounter with Jesus on the Damascus Road he became a new man. He shared his new life in the Epistles he wrote to the various New Testament churches. He encouraged the Philippian believers saying, "Work out your own salvation with fear and trembling; for it is God which work in you both to will and to do of his good pleasure. "Do all things without complaining and disputing" (Philippians 2:12b, 14 NKJV).

John the Baptist

John the Baptist was a forerunner of Jesus Christ, and a good example of humility in leadership. He preached repentance and expressed his humility to the crowd at the Jordan River. He referred to himself as the voice of one crying in the wilderness and declared, "I am not the Christ" (John 1:20b KJV). He let the crowd know that he was no comparison to Jesus saying, "And he preached, saying, there comes One after me who is mightier than I, whose sandal strap I am not worthy to stoop down and loose" (Mark 1:7 NKJV).

John the Baptist told his followers the truth about his mission and exactly what he came to do. He knew he was preparing the way for Jesus the Messiah and was humbly and grateful. He was thankful to be selected for the ministry of a forerunner. He did his ministry so enthusiastically and humbly that Jesus credited John the Baptist as being a true messenger of God, and one of the greatest prophets born of a woman (Matthew 11:10-11 NKJV).

Associate pastors must maintain and magnify their humility by always telling the truth and not wanting to take credit for being someone they are not capable of being. Associate pastors must be aware of the devil and his devices. He will tempt us to lie about our position and try to magnify ourselves. Temptation can be overcome by prayer, mediation, and not being envious or jealous of another we

> **The closer our relationship with Jesus Christ the more like Him we will become. That should always be our goal no matter where we serve in ministry.**

may be called to minister or work with. The closer our relationship with Jesus Christ the more like Him we will become. That should always be our goal no matter where we serve in ministry.

Humility Does Not Make You Weak

In secular society humility is not looked upon as a strength especially in a leadership position. As a matter of fact humility is a characteristic that the world system avoids altogether. The world's way of looking at humility is that a person who is humble is portrayed as being weak minded, timid, easy to persuade or run over.

However, in the spiritual realm humility is a powerful characteristic in godly leadership. It is an indication that a person is under the control of the Holy Spirit and has a true view of God's will for his life. John MacArthur says "A humble man, with a proper view of God will be confident in God's power, committed to God's truth, commissioned by God's will, compelled by God's knowledge and consumed with God's glory."⁵

᛫ Key Points from Chapter 9

- Pride is a symptom that shows a lack of humility.
- The closer our relationship with Jesus Christ the more like Him we will become. That should always be our goal no matter where we serve in ministry.
- "A humble man, with a proper view of God, will be:
  - confident in God's power
  - committed to God's truth
  - commissioned by God's will
  - compelled by God's knowledge
  - consumed with God's glory."⁶

---

5 John MacArthur, Rediscovering Pastoral Ministry (Word Publishing Dallas Texas 1995), 22

6 John MacArthur, Rediscovering Pastoral Ministry (Word Publishing Dallas Texas 1995), 22

CHAPTER 10

BIBLICAL PRINCIPLES FOR LEADERSHIP

God appoints leaders specifically to carry out His missions according to His standards. The biblical principles of leadership have their beginning roots in the Old Testament. In Genesis, Adam was the first person to learn about the biblical principles of leadership. God gave Adam a directive about the trees in the Garden of Eden. He told his wife what tree to eat fruit from and what tree to avoid in the Garden of Eden. She failed miserable. They both were ejected from the Garden of Eden because of their direct disobedience to God's directive to Adam.

In the days of the patriarchs leadership principles were given in the form of covenants. If the patriarchs obeyed these covenants, they were blessed and favored by the people of different nations. If a person was called or appointed as a prophet, priest, king or judge he/she was God's designated leader.

Each position was significant for leading the people of God through a season or event. God gave Moses and the Israelites principles for leadership called the Ten Commandants. Leaders that were chosen and appointed by God were commanded to be obedient and committed to follow these principles faithfully and also to teach them to the people.

> **God appoints leaders specifically to carry out His missions according to His standards.**

In the New Testament church, leadership is to emulate the biblical principles of servant hood as taught and demonstrated by Jesus and the apostles. Jesus came to serve and not be served. He said to His disciples, "And He sat down, called the twelve, and said to them, if anyone desires to be first, he shall be last of all and servant of all" (Mark 9:35 NKJV).

Effective Tools for Leadership

1. *Associate pastors are most effective when they lead in the area of their gifts.*
2. *They must be capable of equipping others for ministry.*
3. *They must set the standard for godliness, morality, productivity, and excellence.*
4. *They must connect and communicate with the people.*
5. *They are not to micro-manage.*
6. *They must give clear instruction.*
7. *They must allow others to perform what they have learned.*
8. *They must be consistence in what they do.*
9. *They must finish what is asked of them in a timely manner.*
10. *They must lead by example.*
11. *They must be compassionate, patient, teachable, and approachable.*
12. *They must not criticize negatively.*

The pathways of the associate pastor are not always easy. The journey can sometimes be filled with humps and bumps. One must not be easily frustrated. Frustration can result in mistakes. Mistakes can cause delays and sometimes misunderstanding. I want to encourage associate pastors not to be easily discouraged, be patient, remain faithful, and steadfast. The Apostle Paul encourages us in in the Lord, "Therefore, my beloved brethren be steadfast, immovable, always abounding in the work of the Lord, knowing that your labor is not in vain in the Lord" (1 Corinthians 15:58 KJV). We must always remember it is God who called us to serve.

These are the biblical principles that associate pastors must always keep in mind:

1. Associate pastors must always pray. Prayer shows you are totally dependent on God. Jesus spoke a parable that taught, "Then He spoke a parable to them that, men ought to always pray, and not lose heart" (Luke 18:1 NKJV). The Apostle Paul says, "Pray without ceasing" (1 Thessalonians 5:17 NKJV).

2. Associate pastors must keep the faith because "without faith is impossible to please God" (Hebrews 11:6a NKJV).
3. Associate pastors must study to show themselves approval unto God (2 Timothy 2:15 KJV).
4. Associate pastors must have characteristics that are controlled by fruit of the Holy Spirit (Galatians 5:22-26 KJV).
5. Associate pastors must be submissive, humble, and respectful to those that have rule over them (Hebrews 13:7 KJV).
6. Associate pastors must know, and faithfully practice biblical principles in their personal and private lives. They must be above reproach, the husband of one wife, temperate, self-controlled, compassionate, not given to drunkenness, not violent, not quarrelsome, not a lover of money, a man who loves and respects his wife and family, and is not a novice. They must live in a way that others

will be encouraged to live their lives in accordance to the principles presented in the Word of God.

According to Robert Radcliffe, we have to struggle to maintain a personal walk with Christ in His Word while ministering to the needs of others.[7]

Associate pastors must have the following solid biblical core beliefs. They must believe that:

God is the creator of the universe.

The Godhead is God the Father, God the Son and God the Holy Spirit.

Jesus is the Son of God, He died for our sins.

The gospel is the death burial and resurrection of Jesus Christ.

God raised Jesus from the dead on the third day.

The gift of eternal life is through faith in Jesus Christ.

---

[7] Robert J Radcliffe, The Effective Ministry as an Associate Pastor (Grand Rapids, Michigan Kregel Publications, 1998) 37.

The Bible is the authority for the church. (No Christian book or commentary can be used in preaching and teaching the Gospel.)

The Bible is the ultimate source for our life's journey.

The sacraments of the church: baptism and communion.

☙ Key Points from Chapter 10

- ☙ God appoints leaders specifically to carry out His missions according to His standards.
- ☙ There are clear biblical principles and core values associate pastors must always keep in mind to be effective servant leaders.
- ☙ We must always remember it is God who called us to serve.

Conclusion

The Bible gives the foundational principles an associate pastor needs in order to learn how to be an effective leader. The Pastoral Epistles of 1 Timothy, 2 Timothy, and Titus play an indispensable role in guiding associate pastors as to what is required of a godly leader. The behaviors of godly leaders are expressions of their character. Character is understood as the evidence that an associate pastor is empowered by the Holy Spirit. While serving in this position, associate pastors must have knowledge, wisdom, and spiritual discernment. They must study as Apostle told Timothy to study to show thyself approval unto God (2 Timothy 2:15 KJV). Associate pastor must read as well "Blessed is he that readeth and they that hear the words of this prophecy and keep those things which are written therein for the time is at hand" (Revelation 1:3 KJV).

The senior pastor is responsible for teaching and training associate pastors for leadership, and preparing them for the challenges that lie ahead in fulfilling the "Great Commission." Associate pastors must not forget their role is to assist the senior pastor in ministering to God's people. They must have a spirit of cooperation. Ministry cannot be done effectively with an unwilling spirit.

This book was written to encourage associate pastors, leaders, and others in the body of Christ to be committed to their divine calling regardless of what position they may hold. Let us embrace our calling and consider, it is a joy to be of service to God and others.

Questions for Review:

Why are biblical principles important for anyone in a leadership position?

Why associate pastors are needed?

Why does character count in ministry?

Why should you understand your role as an associate pastor?

Why should you develop leadership skills?

Why should you pursue godliness?

Why should you keep your focus in ministry?

Why should associate pastor study the scriptures continuously?

What is the importance of faith?

Who empowers associate pastors to serve?

What can cause burnout?

BIBLIOGRAPHY

Engstrom, Ted W. *The Making of a Christian Leader*: Zondervan Publishing House Grand Rapids, Michigan, 1976.

Hawkins, Martin. *The Associate Pastor*: Broadman & Holman Publishers Nashville, Tennessee; 2005.

Hull, Bill. *The Disciple Making Pastor*: Baker Books Grand Rapids, Michigan; 2007.

MacArthur, John. *Rediscovering Pastoral Ministry*: Word Publishing Dallas, Texas; 1995.

Patterson, Richard. *Being a Christian Leader*: Moody Bible Institute Chicago, Illinois, 1985.

Radcliffe, Robert. *Effective Ministry of an Associate Pastor*: Kregel Publications Grand Rapids Michigan1, 1998.

www.ingramcontent.com/pod-product-compliance
Ingram Content Group UK Ltd.
Pitfield, Milton Keynes, MK11 3LW, UK
UKHW022216230426
12048UKWH00016BA/888